This Notebook Belongs To:

____

75379569R00058

Made in the USA
San Bernardino, CA
28 April 2018